Does God Love My Pantyhose?

Short story by...

Stephen Miller

Author's Tranquility Press
ATLANTA, GEORGIA

Copyright © 2024 by Stephen Miller

All rights reserved. No part of this publication may be reproduced, distributed, or transmitted in any form or by any means, including photocopying, recording, or other electronic or mechanical methods, without the prior written permission of the publisher, except in the case of brief quotations embodied in critical reviews and certain other noncommercial uses permitted by copyright law. For permission requests, write to the publisher, addressed "Attention: Permissions Coordinator," at the address below.

Stephen Miller / Author's Tranquility Press
3900 N Commerce Dr. Suite 300 #1255
Atlanta, GA 30344
www.authorstranquilitypress.com

Ordering Information:
Quantity sales. Special discounts are available on quantity purchases by corporations, associations, and others. For details, contact the "Special Sales Department" at the address above.

Does God Love My Pantyhose? / Stephen Miller
Paperback: 978-1-960675-45-3
eBook: 978-1-960675-46-0

CONTENTS

PREFACE 1
CHAPTER ONE 3
CHAPTER TWO 5
CHAPTER THREE 9
CHAPTER FOUR 11
CHAPTER FIVE 17
CHAPTER SIX 22
CHAPTER SEVEN 27
CHAPTER EIGHT 30
CHAPTER NINE 32
CHAPTER TEN 35
CHAPTER ELEVEN 37
CHAPTER TWELVE 41
CHAPTER THIRTEEN 45
CHAPTER FOURTEEN 51
CHAPTER FIFTEEN 54
CHAPTER SIXTEEN 58
CHAPTER SEVENTEEN 60
CHAPTER EIGHTEEN 63
CHAPTER NINTEEN 67
CHAPTER TWENTY 71
CHAPTER TWENTY-ONE 73
CHAPTER TWENTY-TWO 75

PREFACE

"Every man is born as many men and dies as a single one."

—*Martin Heidegger*

Our job is to love others without stopping to inquire whether or not they are worthy.

—*Unknown*

Chapter One

Reggie stood naked in the bathroom, looking at himself in the mirror. The room was much smaller than the bathroom at his previous home. He leaned across the sink and clicked on the mirror lights and carefully applied red lipstick to his thin lips, then rubbed foundation onto his smooth, freshly shaved cheeks. He washed, rinsed, and dried his hands, then gave his eyelashes a flick with dark mascara.

Stepping backward, he admired himself. Will l make a good-looking woman, he wondered? The larger breasts will help, but that'll be later, after the hormone treatments. He combed through his thick blond hair, blowing it dry with a hairdryer. Parted in the middle, it fell straight to his shoulders. A pair of jeans and a white T-shirt were neatly laid out on his bed. He got dressed and pulled a pair of Birkenstocks from under the bed and slipped them onto his bare feet. Today, he decided he would not wear his new gold hoop earrings. With his green canvas backpack slung over his shoulder, he left the apartment wearing a pair of designer's sunglasses and walked downstairs to the ground level. The mailman spotted him coming down. "You're new here," the postman said. "Which apartment is yours?"

"No, I've been here awhile now," Reggie said. "In the same apartment, number 211. Right here." He pointed to his name label on the mailbox. "R. Thorne, right there. That's mine."

The mailman looked confused for a second. "Oh, ok. I guess I didn't realize it was you, Dr. Thorne. I didn't recognize you. Here's your mail." He handed Reggie a magazine and two bills, then went back to sorting mail.

Reggie walked across the parking lot to his old Mazda, looked around, then got in and threw the backpack and mail on the floor, which was already littered with styrofoam cups and plastic lids. Slowly he drove out and headed in the direction of the campus. Along the way he stopped at a minimart for coffee. The clerk rang it up. "Seventy-five cents, Ma'am." Reggie stared at him for a moment, then pulled a wrinkled dollar bill out of his pocket and handed it to the young man, who handed Reggie back a quarter.

Traffic was heavy along the boulevard. Reggie drove in the right lane; a red pickup tailgates him. Then the truck pulled up alongside him. The driver looked at Reggie, then gave him the finger. "Move that piece of shit rice burner, faggot!" the driver yelled, then stepped on the accelerator. The truck lurched ahead.

"Go to hell, redneck," Reggie mumbled to himself.

Traffic moved along slowly as it approached a main intersection. Reggie stopped at the red light, made a right turn, and drove a half mile to the university campus. The faculty parking lot had plenty of empty parking spaces. He pulled into a space at the end of a row, under a maple tree, got out, locked the car, and headed across the blacktop which was already warm from the sun. He quickly walked up the sloped lawn toward the social science center. In front of the main double doors, a group of students were gathered and talking and watching Reggie as he approached. As he passed them, one of the male students said in a loud voice, "What's wrong sister, the closet gets too hot for you? Need a little fresh air?" They all laughed. Reggie disappeared into the building.

Chapter Two

The receptionist greeted him. "Dr. Saville is expecting you. Why don't you go right in." Reggie thanked her and walked down a short hallway and through a door on the left. Every week for the last five months, Reggie Thorne had met for one hour with Collette Saville, a psychiatrist on campus. She had counselled two other men and a woman who were also undergoing sex changes. She was especially intrigued by Reggie Thorne's case.

"Hello Reggie," she said, offering her handshake. "Please make yourself comfortable." She gestured toward two chairs off to the side of the small office. Reggie sat down slowly in the square-backed chair. "I'm having tea, Reggie, orange spice tea. Would you care to join me?"

"Thank you. Yes, I would."

Dr. Saville sat a few feet from him in a matching chair. Between them was a small round table. "Well, how goes the battle?" She smiled at the way doctors sometimes smile at patients, a smile of feigned sympathy.

"Well, it's going pretty well." He straightened himself in the chair. He began to speak, then stopped and sat silently.

After a minute, Dr. Saville said, "Well, we knew, didn't we, that some aspects of this would be simple, and others not so much. "Reggie nodded. "Did something unpleasant happen this morning?"

He looked disgusted. "Oh, you know, the usual crap. Derogatory comments, that kind of stuff. It's funny; I've always thought of university campuses as more tolerant, but..." His voice trailed off.

Dr. Saville stood up. "Tea's ready." She walked over to a small service counter along the wall. "You want to talk about it?"

He looked at her with a pained expression on his face. "A student called me sister." Collette Saville poured tea from a blue and white tea pot into two mugs. "Cream or sugar?" she asked.

"No thanks."

She placed one mug on the small round table next to Reggie, the other she held and walked toward a large window. As she looked out, she said quietly, "Reggie, we have almost completed the first phase of your...I hate to use the word treatment. Perhaps program is a better word. I am now convinced that you are appropriate for gender reassignment. "She sipped the steaming tea. "You're now entering the gender identity phase. This is the time when you and I will explore your degree of stability with female identification. Any misconceptions or misplaced expectations you have will be dealt with during this time." She walked back to her chair, sat down, and looked at Reggie's makeup. "You're wearing makeup. You must've known because we discussed it and expected it. We knew, didn't we, that it would cause a reaction from some people."

After taking a sip of the tea, he noticed his lipstick had left a bright red smudge on the rim of the mug. "But I want to wear it. I like it. I like the way it makes me look and feel."

"Of course, you do," she said quickly. "I'm not for one minute suggesting that you do not wear it." Her brown eyes fixed on his thin face. She smiled her gentle half smile. "In a few years, you'll look back on this difficult time and be glad you had the strength to do what your heart told you to do."

Reggie sighed. "Yes. I just wish it could all happen much faster. The chairman of the department is trying to be supportive. Some of the other professors are not saying anything to my face. "

She nodded. "Well, put yourself in their position. They're watching you change from a conservative male to a female. They hired a male professor who is changing into a woman."

Reggie chuckled. "It is rather bizarre, I suppose."

"You see, they think you're psychologically unstable, confused. Some of them probably think you're gay. They don't realize that you are emotionally and psychologically a female."

Reggie stood up and walked over to the window and looked down at the rows of maple trees that lined the parking lot and the walkway leading up to the wide steps in front of the building. A large American flag hung limply in the summer heat.

Collette Saville noticed the tight jeans he was wearing, and hesitated, not sure whether or not to ask her next question. "Is the physical part still bothersome?"

He looked at her. "You mean the erections?"

"Yes, and the penis in general. It's going to be awhile before the surgery."

"I don't like it, but it's still a source of erotic pleasure. I sometimes wake up in the middle of the night with an erection, and I want sex right then and there. The funny thing is, it's not during an erotic dream. It just happens."

Dr. Saville walked over and stood next to him and placed her hand on his arm. She could tell he was frustrated by the masculine sexual stirrings. "I believe when we begin the estrogen treatments there will be fewer erections. Until then, I can think of no reason why you can't masturbate to relieve yourself."

He looked at her. "I don't want to."

"Ok," she said softly.

Chapter Three

After his appointment with Dr. Saville, Reggie gave two lectures, then retreated to his small office. The lectures went well, the classes were full, and the level of student participation had been good. But he was distracted by a letter he received from the mother of a student: "My daughter is withdrawing from your European history class, Dr. Thorne. I am thoroughly disgusted and quite surprised that such a fine university would employ a professor whose lifestyle is clearly out of step with the average student's family. Signed, A Normal Heterosexual Parent." The letter had upset him and affected his ability to concentrate during the lectures.

The phone rang. It was the cheerful voice of his daughter. "Hi Daddy."

"Hi Sweetheart. I'm glad you called."

"Are you still coming over?"

"Yes, of course. Did you think I wouldn't?"

"I just miss you and hope you come over every day. Mom wants to talk to you."

Reggie stood up. This, he thought, might not be too pleasant. "Hello Caitlin, how are you?"

Caitlin Thorne was a stunningly beautiful woman. Her mother was of Irish descent, her father was half Hispanic and half Black. Her brown eyes were wide, her tan skin flawless, her dark umber hair cut in a short Afro.

"Well, as good as can be expected, I suppose." She sounded tired." Most of the neighbors are avoiding me now. I see them at the market. They don't say much. Same thing with friends at church."

There was a long silent pause. Finally, he said, "Sabrina asked if I was still coming over on Saturday. "

"Well, are you?"

"I told her I would."

"Do us a favor, would you please? Nothing weird, ok? No lipstick, no eyeshadow. Try to look straight if it isn't asking too much. I mean, we have to live here, you know. We're trying to deal with this. I'd appreciate it if you'd keep that in mind."

"Of course, I'll keep it in mind."

"Good. What time do you plan to be here?"

"Around noon."

"Ok. Here, Sabrina wants to say goodbye."

"Daddy, I love you and I miss you. Bring me a surprise, ok?"

"Ok sweetheart. I'll see you Saturday." He hung up the phone and felt lonely and empty.

Chapter Four

On Saturday Reggie drove slowly up Valley View Drive, being careful to avoid the children and dogs that would undoubtedly be playing outdoors on a warm June morning. Many of the homes in the neighborhood were occupied by university faculty members and their families. Some, like the Thornes, had grade-school kids; Sabrina was ten and finishing fifth grade. Other families had teenagers who drove too fast on the narrow hillside streets.

Dr. and Mrs. Reginald E. Thorne purchased their home soon after he was hired as a professor of European history at an annual salary of seventy-nine thousand dollars, plus additional compensation for teaching the summer quarter. Mrs. Thorne's part-time annual income of nineteen thousand, earned as a contributing editor for two national magazines, helped the young family enjoy a level of comfort that included annual vacations, two cars, private school for Sabrina, and, perhaps most important, provided extra cash for Caitlin to indulge her love for contemporary Russian art. On the walls of their brick, Tudor style house hung nearly eighty thousand dollars' worth of oils by three leading Russian painters. She hadn't actually paid that much; Less than half that. Most of the works were obtained through a broker who was helping finance the departure of two artists from Russia.

Reggie steered his old Mazda along the narrow road, past the small park and playground where he had often taken Sabrina to play. Turning up the steep driveway while shifting into low gear, he parked in his old spot next to Caitlin's van and walked up the brick stairs to the front door. The top half of the Dutch door was open, and he could see Sabrina in the living room off to the right of the foyer. She heard her father approach and turned around.

"Daddy!" she said in a loud, enthusiastic voice. "I've been waiting for you." She hugged her father around the waist. "Can we go see Free Willy?"

He smiled and kissed the top of her head. "Haven't we seen that one?"

"Yes, but Daddy, it's playing today at the matinee." Her father kissed her again on the top of her head and smelled her clean hair and scalp.

"Well, let's talk about it. I thought since it's such a nice day you might like to go out to the creek in the state park and catch crawdads, take a picnic, ride the bikes."

"I can help make a picnic, can't I Mom?" the child said to her mother who had entered the foyer. "Hi Reg," she said. She had always called him Reg. Not Reggie, not Reginald, just Reg. Then, referring to his straight appearance, she mouthed the words Thank You. His hair was pulled back neatly in a ponytail and his clothing was conservative. No makeup.

Caitlin Thorne often appeared to be looking for something. It was a habit that Reggie found quite distracting and annoying. Her facial expressions were like one would have while browsing through a bookstore or searching for a bathroom in an unfamiliar house. More often than not, her brown eyes were wide open, like a Keane painting. Her head turned jerkily to the left, then to the right. She usually looked beyond what was directly in front of her. Even in her own home, her own kitchen, the contents of which she had long ago memorized, she seemed to be searching for the misplaced paprika, or the missing bay leaves.

A model during her teen years, she was now a thirty-four-year-old beauty who turned the heads of men and women alike. Her husband, Dr. Reginald Thorne, PhD., had many times looked on with pride during social gatherings while friends and colleagues would surround his gorgeous wife in an effort to engage her in conversation, or simply to get a closer look. Her figure, after the birth of her child, was lovely: Full breasts, smoothly rounded hips, twenty-nine-inch waist, perfectly sculpted arms, and legs. Her friends told her she was an above-average tennis player.

Reggie looked at her, taking in her beauty for several seconds. "You look great," he said.

She ignored the compliment. "Everything ok over at the U?" she asked.

He looked her up and down. She was wearing a white tank top and navy jogging shorts. "Yes, everything is fine," he lied. "Hey! How 'bout the three of us going for a picnic out at the state park? Take the swimsuits?"

"No, you two go," she answered. "I have some things planned that I need to get done before Monday. The new Assistant Pastor may stop by later." She said she needed to finish an article before the deadline. It would be the cover story, the editor promised her.

Reggie watched her facial expressions as she spoke. Though good-looking, she now had a somewhat hardened expression, borne out of financial pressure and uncertainty caused by her husband's extraordinary behavior. The recent turn of events had taken a huge toll on her happiness and contentment. She was, he knew, no longer willing to endure the humiliation of being married to, and seen in public with, a husband who had decided to become a female, and look and live like a female, and undergo psychiatric counselling which necessarily preceded the estrogen treatments, the growing breasts, the legal change of identification for employment, insurance, and driver's license, and, finally, the reconstructive surgery to remove the penis and testes and replaced them with a surgically constructed vagina.

No! Absolutely not! Caitlin had told him in no uncertain terms that she would not participate in what she had termed his 'charade,' his 'little fantasy,' his 'whatever the hell it is you're doing to your life and ours.'

"Sabrina, why don't you get your bike out of the garage and wheel it out in my car. I'm going to talk to mommy for a minute." The child walked out and down the brick stairway to the garage.

Caitlin looked at her soon-to-be ex-husband. "So, found a roommate yet?"

"I think so. I've interviewed several prospects. I'll be making a final decision by tomorrow evening. I want to wrap this thing up."

"You're telling them, aren't you, about your change? I mean, you can't very well just spring it on them after they've moved in."

"I have no intention of springing it on them. I tell them up front that mine is an alternative lifestyle."

Caitlin scoffed. "Well, that can mean different things to different people, Reg."

"Yes, that's true," he said as he walked around the living room. "By the way, I'd like to have this piece that my parents gave us," he said, pointing at an antique China cabinet along the wall in the corner.

"Nothing leaves this house until my attorney, and I decide what's what," she snapped back.

"Your attorney!" he said with contempt.

"That's right, my attorney, she said, her voice raised. "He's been a great help to me, helping me chart my future."

"Charting your future?" he asked sarcastically, feigning laughter.

Caitlin walked up to him and stood directly in front of him, their noses almost touching. "Do you remember the stuff I went through to convince my family that you were the right man for me? Do you recall my dad's insistence that I marry a Catholic, and raise my child in the Catholic Church and have a Catholic wedding? Remember? But no! You wouldn't have it. You insisted on a Protestant wedding! One short prayer! During our wedding ceremony, my dad and mom sat there like statues, humiliated because their only daughter got married outside the faith. At first you agreed to a Catholic wedding, but then at the last minute you changed your mind. My mother cried!" Caitlin began to weep quietly. "My brothers were furious with me for agreeing with you. Do you remember? They threatened to come to our house and kick your ass! I shouldn't have stopped them." She went into the downstairs bathroom and got a tissue and wiped her eyes.

She continued. "Have you noticed that they rarely call? It's because of you! I send them pictures of our daughter and guess what? No response! "Reggie nodded his head. "Four weeks after our wedding, my dad had a fatal heart attack! He died never understanding why I didn't find a nice man in the Catholic church." She went on for another five minutes. 'Look, Sabrina and I need a secure future, and I can't plan it by myself. Oh, I suppose I could if forced to, but I have professional help, and I'm damn glad to have it. Her voice was louder now. You've decided to walk away from our life and plans, and I guess I can deal with that. But I'm staying put."

"We'll give you a medal," he said sarcastically.

"What the hell does that mean?" she shot back contemptuously.

"Nothing, Caitlin," he said. He walked over to the bookshelf and looked at no book in particular. Turning toward his wife, he looked wounded. "Look, I'm trying to be honest with you, with our daughter, with myself, with life. This isn't what is supposed to be. I don't identify with any of this," he said, referring to his body.

Caitlin Thorne looked at him with an expression of pity, amazement, and disgust. "Well, it sounds like you're going all the way with this thing. Should be very interesting explaining all this to Sabrina."

"Someday she'll understand," he said quietly.

"Bullshit! She will be teased at school. She'll be humiliated, mocked. "Caitlin began imitating the mocking: "How's your dad, Sabrina? Oh, I forgot, he's now your mother, but you already have a mother. So now you have two mothers. Gee, that's different." She was practically shouting, but stopped when she heard her daughter come up the stairs.

Reggie went over to the Dutch door and opened the lower half for his daughter. "Sabrina, let's stop at the deli on the way out and get some of that salad you like, and a couple hoagy sandwiches."

"Ok Dad. My bike's ready."

Reggie looked at his watch. "Let's go then. I'll have her back home by suppertime." They walked out into the sunshine, loaded the bike into the trunk, and drove off.

Chapter Five

In his quest to understand the various aspects of his transformation from male to female, Reggie Thorne had begun developing a small circle of friends who had either made the change themselves or were related to someone who had. Following the afternoon with Sabrina, Reggie planned to attend a barbeque at the home of a couple he'd met through his psychiatrist. Merrill and Bridget Wells were an interesting couple, to say the least. Merrill was in the same phase of his transformation as Reggie. As the owner of three successful shoe stores, Merrill was well-known in the community and knew many of his customers by name. His father and uncle had owned the stores previously and Merrill had worked in the stores since he was fourteen. Now, 25 years later, Merrill Wells was charging undaunted into his sex change, even appearing in public dressed like a conservative businesswoman.

This, however, caused a bit of a problem with some of his older customers, who hadn't purchased shoes anywhere else for years. So, to avoid dealing with the inevitable reactions of his customers, he stopped going into the stores. Bridget took over the day-to-day management responsibilities.

Unlike Caitlin Thorne, Bridget Wells did not insist on a divorce, nor was she humiliated by her husband's extraordinary behavior. Quite the contrary. She rather fancied him as a player, as she put it, "a player on the stage of life." And, not lacking a flair for the dramatic, she seemed quite curious about what this life change would bring to her. As luck would have it, Merrill and Bridget were nearly the same height and weight, so Merrill fit quite comfortably into his wife's clothes, often raiding her side of the closet!

Even more extraordinary than this was the fact that Merrill desired sex not with men but with women, indeed, his own wife. Bridget, herself quite the free-thinker, welcomed this bizarre twist in their marriage.

The Wells' lived on two acres, a mile south of town. Reggie found their farmhouse with little effort. The tall evergreens that circled the place offered a good deal of seclusion, and also blocked the summer winds. When Reggie got there, it was nearly 100 degrees. He hoped they would have air conditioning and the common sense to stage this little get-together indoors. They did.

He parked near the house at the end of a long dirt road. As he approached the front door, it swung open. "Reggie," a dark-haired woman said enthusiastically. "I'm Bridget. Please join us indoors. The heat is stifling."

"I agree," Reggie said. "Thank you. "

"You found us with no trouble, I hope. Do you like to be called Reggie or Reginald?"

"I'm not sure at this point. Reggie is fine for now, and the directions Dr. Saville gave me were easy to follow."

"Please make yourself comfortable. I'll tell Merrill you're here. Not sure if he heard you drive up."

The living room was sparsely furnished with natural grain furniture, several large cacti, American Indian blankets on two walls and an extraordinary landscape covering one entire wall with an image of a desert sunrise or sunset, Reggie wasn't sure which. He found the décor interesting, especially one striking feature: An entire wall appeared to be made of large pieces of blue and green slate. In the middle of the wall was a round, six-foot diameter window that looked out onto the deck and hot tub, and beyond to a thicket of blackberries. A large terrarium extended half the length of one wall and was home to three iguanas with long spiked tails. Reggie looked at them. They were standing quite still.

He wasn't prepared for the grand entrance of Merrill Wells. What he saw next was nothing short of amazing. The man of the house appeared dressed in a full-length white linen grand boubou. On his tan feet were brown leather sandals. The boubou was almost sheer and underneath he wore white underpants. His dark hair was thick and combed back in a high pompadour, and the back was long enough to drop to the base of his neck. On each earlobe hung a large silver hoop and he was wearing red lipstick and was perfectly tanned. Reggie glanced quickly at his flat chest.

"I'm Merrill," he said, extending his perfectly manicured right hand. In his arms was a large gray Persian cat with steel blue eyes and long white whiskers. The animal stared intently at Reggie. "I thought you'd like to see my pussy," he said with a mischievous grin. Bridget, upon hearing the double entendre, burst into shrieking laughter.

"Merrill," she said, "sometimes you are such a bad boy."

Reggie laughed uncomfortably and blushed a bright pink. He reached to pet the cat. With lightning speed, the cat's right paw snapped toward Reggie, but he quickly withdrew his hand to avoid the needle-sharp claws. Merrill put the cat on the floor.

"I'm Reggie Thorne," he said, thrusting his right hand toward his host in a very masculine handshake gesture, before realizing that he wasn't shaking hands with a man but with a soon-to-be woman. He quickly let up on the firm handshake that he had used all his adult life and gently shook Merrill's hand.

"How do you do, Reggie. I'm delighted you could be here. I would guess that you and I have many things to talk about." He smelled of fine perfume.

Bridget Wells was beaming, obviously enjoying the spectacle of her husband. She moved over and stood in front of him, wrapping both arms around his waist. "Honey, why don't I offer our guest some refreshment?

She turned toward Reggie. "What may I offer you in the way of beverage?"

Still a bit dumbfounded by his host and hostess, Reggie replied, "Well, I would love a glass of wine."

"We have a dry white and a delicious Merlot."

"The white will be fine."

"The same please," Merrill said. Bridget disappeared into the kitchen.

Momentarily, she reentered the living room carrying a wine bottle and a small tray with three wine glasses. She set them on a glass-top table, left the room and returned with an ice bucket that she put next to the table. After pouring the wine, she stuck the bottle into the chipped ice.

Merrill handed one glass to Reggie, who looked admiringly at the golden liquid. He lifted the glass to his nose and smelled the pleasant, fruity bouquet.

"To changes," Merrill said, lifting the glass in a toast, his mouth breaking into a wide grin. He laughed, not a masculine beer-swilling horse laugh but a sweet, feminine chuckle.

"Yes," Reggie said enthusiastically, "Yes, to the rest of our lives. May our days be many and fulfilling." With that, they clinked the glasses and sipped the wine. It was cool and dry and refreshing. Reggie took another drink, this one larger than the first.

"It's an Oregon chardonnay," Merrill said. "Ponzi Vineyards. Delicious, isn't it?"

"Very."

"Well, enjoy. Please drink your fill. There's plenty more."

Reggie looked down at the dusty sandals he'd been wearing all day, and the khaki shorts and blue golf shirt. "I guess I could've dressed up a little more. I wasn't sure what the evening dress code would be."

"Don't be silly, Reggie," Bridget reassured him, touching his arm. "You look great. The unisex look. I like it myself. As you can probably tell, Merrill and I wear the same size in almost everything, and we share our clothes. Since Merrill began cross dressing, I decided to cross dress occasionally, too. That boubou he's wearing is mine, or rather, ours. I often wear some of his clothes."

The evening went on that way. They discussed clothes, books, movies, art and architecture, politics, and religion. Reggie thought they had deliberately avoided the subjects of sex and cross dressing in public. Probably just as well, he thought. It appeared that Merrill Wells was a step or two ahead of him in the sex change process. The barbequed chicken breasts were delicious, served with wild rice and fresh green beans from Merrill's garden. They capped the evening with brandy in snifters. Later, Reggie droves home to his empty, lonely apartment.

Chapter Six

A daffodil yellow sun rose over the mountains through a low fog at six-thirty the next morning and Reggie was up and dressed to watch it. Today he would make a final decision on a roommate. He had already decided he wanted a female. Of the three young ladies he had met through his advertising, one named Malka Silverman had impressed him particularly. In her late twenties, she had been working as a dental hygienist for four years at an office near the university. He expected her to call that day before noon. The other two applicants would be calling later in the afternoon. He hoped Malka would rent the room so he could tell the other two that the room was no longer available.

He drank a small glass of apple juice, put on jogging shorts and a sweat shirt, and went out for a run. Though still early, the summer air was quite warm and he knew the afternoon would be hot. He jogged slowly toward the campus, along the boulevard until he got to the south end of the football field, cut across the lawn onto the track, two laps around the field, then back to his apartment.

He ate an orange and a bowl of raisin bran standing up because he didn't yet have a kitchen table or chairs. In the living room were two overstuffed chairs that he picked up at a garage sale. Between them was a small square wooden table. That, he thought, would be a good place to sit and discuss things with Malka. A tall bookshelf, also from a garage sale, took up nearly half of the longest wall. On the floor was a CD player and two small speakers. His bedroom furnishings consisted of a box spring and mattress, and a lamp and his personal computer and a printer on a small wooden desk. Later in the day he would check out a couple second-hand shops to find a kitchen table and chairs.

While he was showering, he heard the phone ring. He stepped out of the shower and wrapped a towel around his waist and walked dripping wet into the kitchen and answered the phone. It was Malka. Have you made a decision about a roommate, she asked. Yes, he said, but there are a few things we need to discuss before we finalize this. He asked if they could meet for lunch. They decided to meet at Saul's Bagel Shop at noon. After they got off the phone, Reggie got back in the shower. Right away he was sorry he'd suggested Saul's. The bagels were fresh every day, and they served great bagel sandwiches, but the place was always packed. He definitely didn't want to discuss his intention to change genders while sitting in a crowded café. He finished his shower, dried off, put on shorts and a white t-shirt, read part of the Sunday paper, then left to meet Malka. He walked the five blocks to Saul's. It was hot already and what he really wanted was an iced tea. Saul's had twelve small tables, and there were just two women there having coffee. This might work out after all, he thought.

Malka Silverman had described herself as five feet tall with short dark hair. She'd be wearing a short-sleeved pullover shirt and white shorts and sandals. She was easy to spot when she walked in at exactly noon. Reggie appreciated her being on time. "Malka," he said standing up to shake hands with her.

"Hi Reggie," she answered in a clipped but not unfriendly voice.

"I should've asked you if you like bagels" he said as they both sat down. "Would you rather go to McDonalds?" She said yes, so they walked two blocks to McDonalds. It was crowded, so they ordered burgers and fries, and a lemonade and iced tea and walked over to a shady spot on campus and sat on a bench. While Malka ate, Reggie talked.

"The ad I ran in the newspaper used the words Alternative Lifestyle. You probably noticed that."

With a mouthful of fries, Malka asked," Are you gay?"

Reggie pondered the question for a few seconds. "Would it be a problem if I was?" She shook her head and said no.

He wondered if he should just drop the bomb on her. He decided to. "Would it be a problem for you if I was transsexual"?

He could tell she was curious now. "Is that like running around the apartment in women's clothing?" she asked. She took a bite of her cheeseburger.

Reggie chuckled. "Malka, I believe I'm a female. "She stopped chewing and stared at him. "There was a biological error made that trapped me in a male body." Well, he thought, that certainly got her attention. "The wearing of women's clothes is part of it." Malka, by this time, had stopped eating and put what was left of her lunch back in the bag. She was hanging on every word.

"There's more. I'm currently going through counselling in preparation for treatments and surgery which will…" he paused, "which will physically change me from a male to female."

Malka sat in stone silence, After what seemed like a very long pause, she asked, "Are you going to change your name?"

"Probably. Maybe to Regina."

"Do your parents know about this?"

He laughed. "No, not exactly."

"You're going to have to learn how to pee sitting down." They both laughed. "You'll have to learn a whole new way of doing things. It's going to be strange for you. When I was a toddler, my parents got me a little pink plastic toddler toilet. I've been peeing sitting down for a long time." She thought for a moment. "What kind of work do you do? Didn't you tell me you're a teacher?"

He pointed to the social sciences building. "I teach right over there."

"What will happen to your job?"

"Good question. I am hoping to keep my job. I suppose if I get fired I can move to Vegas and make a living playing black jack. I have a college buddy who lives there. He'll let me sleep on his couch."

They sat in silence for a while. Reggie thought about his job at the university. Tomorrow he would have three lectures, two in the morning, one in the afternoon. "Well, this is all very interesting, I must say," Malka said finally. "You are certainly a nice-looking man." She had heard of people being trapped in the wrong body. "I've always thought of myself as fairly open-minded. I've heard of people doing what you're thinking about doing."

Reggie interrupted her. "I'm not thinking about it. The final decision was made quite a while ago." He said firmly, "Look, if you want to reconsider for a couple days, that's fine."

"No, I don't need to reconsider. If you think I'd make a good roommate, I'm definitely willing to try it." She was becoming more comfortable with the idea and dug into her McDonald's bag and retrieved a few cold fries and stuffed them in her mouth.

"Ok, good. But please understand that I realize the extremely unusual nature of what I'm doing. If it becomes intolerable for you, if it's just too weird, I'll understand."

Malka was smiling and munching on cold fries. "Well, I'll explain it to my friends. They'll be stopping over occasionally. How long have you known your wife?" she asked. "Did you date for a long time before you got married? I mean, was your relationship with her ever normal?"

Reggie smiled. "Well, that's an interesting question. I met her sister, Erin, before I knew Caitlin. The three of us went to the same university. Erin and I began dating around Christmastime, and the following Spring I got her pregnant. That was also when I met Caitlin, and she and I hit it off right away. "

"Oh my God," Malka said. "Did her family know that she was pregnant? What did Caitlin think about it? Oh my God!" she said again.

"Let's talk about it another time," he said.

Malka took a checkbook from her back pocket, and asked about the first month's rent and deposit, and when she could move in. He told her to move in as soon as possible, and the deposit was already paid, so just the first month's rent is all that's required. She could give him a check the day she moved in, he said, and the phone and utilities are split evenly. That settled, they walked back to the bagel shop where Malka had left her car. Reggie walked home.

Chapter Seven

The walk home was hot, the summer sun beating down and making the sidewalk a hotplate under his feet. He was glad to have the roommate matter settled. It would help him financially to reduce his portion of the rent. Most of his paycheck went to his wife for the mortgage, Caitlin's car payment and insurance, Sabrina's school tuition, his 401k, child support, living expenses, and the ten percent he promised to continue putting into savings. He also paid $170 per month for his vehicle, which would be paid off in five months. Caitlin had given him a Past Due Notice for the Homeowner's Association dues, and he wasn't sure exactly when he could pay it.

But, even with a roommate, he was strapped financially, which was a serious problem, because he couldn't afford the silk blouses and pretty dresses that he wanted to wear. He envied Merrill and Bridget Wells' ability and willingness to swap clothing. Reggie thought about Sabrina. How would he deal with her? She really had no idea about the change in her father's life. The child understood that last summer, her mother explained to her that mommy and daddy were going to live separately for a few months. She had heard her parents quarrel a few times, which upset her and brought her to tears.

The first quarrel occurred one evening when Reggie, with Caitlin's permission, put on one of her dresses and a pair of her shoes, neither of which fit well. He also put on lipstick and other makeup. The straight-laced Caitlin allowed this "bit of silliness" as she referred to it, only in the privacy of their bedroom. Because she was a good deal shorter and had a curvy figure, the clothes hung on him ridiculously. His suggestion that he buy a few outfits that actually fit him was greeted with shock. His wife called it a preposterous idea, "We can't afford for you to go out and waste good money on dresses, " is what she said. Besides, she continued, "it's not right, it's not normal for a man to wear a dress. Why would you want to want to wear a dress?" I suppose, she said in a mocking way, "we could find you a kilt and bagpipes, if you'd be willing to learn an Irish jig to entertain our friends." She laughed at him and he realized she didn't have a clue how he felt.

Another late night argument, after which he spent the night on the couch, was a result of Reggie asking his wife to stimulate him with her vibrator, or rather, their vibrator, which he had bought for her several months before. Again, Caitlin didn't know how to interpret the request. So, she got out of bed. "I'm sorry, this doesn't turn me on at all," she said as she walked into the bathroom. Reggie, at that point very turned on, thought he probably should have let her get on top of him and ride his erection to climax. She enjoyed being on top. But, by then it was too late. Later, when he tried to discuss it, they quarreled.

The whole issue of the vibrator had not set well with Caitlin. Oh, she appreciated it alright, and had enjoyed many terrific orgasms with it. She kept it conveniently located in a bedside table along with scented and flavored lubricants. But she preferred a more traditional sex act with her husband, and settled for the buzzing plastic phallus only as a last resort. Bringing the vibrator into their home was in itself a major event. Reggie couldn't bring it into the house until Sabrina was in bed, and, even then, Caitlin refused for a week to even look at it. Finally, after several glasses of wine, she consented to take the device out and inspect it. But Reggie was sorry he'd ever brought it home. It seemed to make Caitlin as angry as it made her hot. Afterward, after playing with the vibrator and having two powerful orgasms, she would berate him for his "non-performance," as she put it. "I guess I should be thankful for modern technology and Eveready batteries," she said coldly.

When Reggie finally announced to his wife that he was transsexual, the ceiling caved in. Hell, hath no fury like a woman whose spouse decides to change horse's mid-stream. That was the beginning of the end.

Chapter Eight

Caitlin had asked the new Assistant Pastor to stop by to discuss the various church programs for youth. She also wanted to pick his brain on the topic of transsexualism among church membership.

"I would do everything within my power to discourage that sort of behavior, particularly within the parameters of a Christian marriage," the pastor told Caitlin. "There is no scriptural support for it. But one doesn't have to be a church-goer to recognize that it flies in the face of nature. God gave man and woman a reproductive system with a specific purpose in mind." He asked Caitlin if her husband is a believer.

"I always thought so. He was raised in a Christian family. They went to church every Sunday. I think his dad was a Deacon or Elder."

The young Pastor shook his head. "Please have him give me a call anytime. "He handed Caitlin his business card. " I can be reached at the church or at home." He turned and headed for the door. "Your daughter needs to be considered as well, Mrs. Thorne. I'm sure your husband has thought about that."

Caitlin took a step toward him. "Pastor, am I wrong to divorce my husband? Tell me honestly." She thought about her family; Her parents, her brothers, her sister Erin who Reggie knocked up and who later married a nice Catholic man. There were no divorces in her family. She would be the first.

"Mrs. Thorne, your husband is responsible for the

predicament you are in."

"Does God still love me? Does He love my husband when he wears women's clothing?"

"Yes, Mrs. Thorne, God loves both of you." He turned and walked out to his car and drove off.

Chapter Nine

That evening it cooled off quite a bit. Reggie opened the front door and the windows in the bedrooms to let the cool evening breeze blow through. Malka Silverman had called to say she'd be moving her things the day after tomorrow. Was the apartment air conditioned, she asked. No. Well, her parents had a small air conditioner that fit in a window, that they were no longer using. They'd probably let her bring it along. That would be fine, Reggie told her. She also had a waterbed, and would it be ok for her to bring it? No problem, he said, but then later he realized it could be a problem because the rental agreement specifically stated no waterbeds. If it leaks and the water seeps through into the unit below, then we'll be evicted and liable for damages. All of a sudden, this roommate idea that had seemed so great before was beginning to stink a bit. Well, he thought he'd try it and see how it goes.

For two of his classes the next day, Reggie had planned a discussion of the Mikhail Gorbachev years, the years of *glasnost* and *perestroika* in the Soviet Union. He had met the Russian leader twice, once in Moscow and once in Washington, D.C. when Gorbachev was visiting President Reagan. It was one of his favorite parts of the class, because of the great historical significance and the transition that had taken place in the U.S.S.R. Reggie viewed Gorbachev as one of the greatest leaders of the century for his bravery and determination to usher in a new era for his countrymen.

Reggie, in a personal way, could relate to the idea of sweeping out the old and replacing it with the new. More than anything, he wanted to close the chapter on his former self, his male self, and begin writing a new chapter of who he really was. He wanted to, needed to, dress in women's clothing while working, while at home or running errands, and all the time. The unisex look that Bridget Wells had referred to be a cop out. The wholewheat look, jeans and fisherman knit sweaters and sandals or Birkenstocks was ok but not particularly feminine. For that reason, he felt he was not only born in the wrong body, but also in the wrong era. If he could turn the clock back to the Forties or Fifties, when men dressed like men and ladies like ladies, maybe he would've been happier.

But now, he would just have to make the best of it. So again, this week, he would wear lipstick and mascara and carefully brush and spray his hair. He went into the bathroom and looked at his lips and realized that in a few days he'd be sharing the bathroom with another person. Would he be sharing makeup with Malka, he wondered? He carefully applied a very dark red lipstick. Although he'd done it now dozens of times, it still required time and effort to put it on straight. There was the base makeup, the flesh tone stuff that ladies put on their cheeks, nose, forehead, and down around the chin. If you looked carefully, you could usually see where the makeup ended, and the natural skin started. Reggie would avoid that, he thought to himself. The mascara seemed simple enough to apply.

He looked at his hands. Nature hadn't dealt him a pair of big hands and fat fingers, but his knuckles were hairy, as were the back of his hands. He would shave it off. He'd also have to begin paying more attention to his nails, let them grow longer, and paint his toenails. He recalled shaking hands with Merrill Wells and how it was like shaking hands with a woman. His own handshake, the classic John Wayne handshake where you thrust your right hand out like a karate move and pump the hell out of the other guy's hand, well, that would have to change, too. He thought back to the dinner at Merrill and Bridget Wells' home.

He remembered the double entendre of Merrill's pussy. Reggie wondered what he would look like someday. He wanted one just like Caitlin's, soft to the touch with soft curly hair. What about clitoris? And would his new vagina be moist and have muscles like Caitlin's, able to grip a penis during intercourse? So many unknowns.

The marriage of Merrill and Bridget was interesting. Both appeared totally accepting of Merrill's pending sex change. Reggie wondered if they were now having normal intercourse. And, if so, how does that square with having a sex change. And after Merrill's surgery, would they be considered lesbians? That night, as Reggie went to bed, his mind was spinning.

Chapter Ten

In the morning, Reggie was up before six. His first lecture wasn't until nine, but he wanted to shave and shampoo and have plenty of time to put on makeup. During the night, he had awakened and realized that, to a great extent, he was alone in the world. Yes, there was Dr. Saville and Merrill and Bridget to turn to for support, but out in the day-to-day world, he was alone. This realization was both frightening and liberating. He took a long shower, shampooed, and applied lots of conditioners to make his hair shiny. Then he shaved twice with a new razor for the smoothest shave possible. After the estrogen treatments begin, his facial hair would start to disappear. The estrogen would also cause his testicles to atrophy and body fat to redistribute. His hips would curve, and his breasts enlarge.

Malka Silverman had all her personal belongings moved in and was now a legal occupant of the apartment, having had her name added to the lease agreement. Everything was moving along smoothly.

The following Sunday evening, something extraordinary happened. Reggie was sitting on his bed reading and Malka walked in slowly, wearing a tank top and bikini panties, smiling and with a slight slur in her words. "Hi Reggie. Whatcha doing?" She had a glass of wine in one hand, sat on the edge of his bed, and placed the other hand on his leg just above his knee. She took a sip of the wine. "Reggie, your leg feels really nice. Firm. Hairy but not too hairy." Her hand moved up closer to his crotch.

Reggie removed his reading glasses and closed the book. Malka's fingertips playfully caressed his leg and slid under his khaki shorts. For the first time in a long while, his penis began to swell. Malka noticed the bulge in his shorts and wrapped her slender fingers around his hardening penis. "I want to fuck you now, while you still have a cock. Please Reggie!" She slid her panties off and climbed onto the bed next to him. "I'm very wet, Reggie," she said. "Take your shorts off. Here, I'll help you." She lowered the zipper and quickly unbuttoned the shorts and, with Reggie's assistance, removed them and flung them onto the floor. He was wearing no underpants, and she quickly climbed on top of him and lowered herself onto his rigid penis and let out a moan. "That feels so good," she whispered, moving up and down faster. Her eyes were closed, her mouth open as her breathing became more labored. "Oh!" she moaned, "I'm gonna cum fast!" Her hips were pounding up and down, Reggie's hands on her waist. She let out another very long moan as her climax shook through her body. Momentarily, she laid down on top of him and closed her eyes.

He was still rock hard inside her. He laid there with her in his arms. Staring at the ceiling, he enjoyed the closeness of her perspiring body. Soon, he closed his eyes and fell asleep.

Chapter Eleven

The history lectures were going well, and the classes were full. There were just a couple dropouts, and most of the students joined in the discussions. Reggie had missed a recent Friday lecture to fly to Washington, D.C. to confer with state department officials regarding the future of the incoming Russian president Boris Yeltsen. For the meeting he wore a dark conservative suit, a short wig, and no makeup. Later that day, he would try to visit with a college friend who was working in the administration of President Bill Clinton.

Reggie was distracted by his apparent hypocrisy regarding his appearance. He and Dr. Saville had recently discussed gender identity and testing his ability and willingness to live as a woman. And, although he tried to put it out of his mind, he was annoyed that he had allowed himself to be seduced by Malka Silverman. Yes, he had enjoyed it, and wasn't confused about what it meant: A cheap thrill, a quickie sexual encounter. He had enjoyed pleasuring Malka more than himself. His mind wandered back to the evening they were together. He smiled. She's a hot little number. He had enjoyed the intimate contact, something he'd gone without for a long time.

Looking back, he now saw Caitlin as a rather cold, distant woman whose own personal agenda often superseded the family's. Caitlin's needs and wants were at the center of her little universe. It had been that way ever since he met her. While he was in grad school, he could never understand why a woman of her charm and beauty would be interested in a bookworm history major doctorate candidate like him. Even his own mother had warned Caitlin that he wasn't as much fun as he used to be, always reading, spending every extra moment in the library, spending what little money he had on books. Whenever his mom packed up the family and headed to the beach or park for a picnic, there would be Reggie with his nose in a book. Reginald, for heaven's sake, put down that book and go play with your brother, his mother would say. Go have some fun! And he'd answer, "But I am having fun. This is a great book!" Then his mother would sigh and go back to her crochet or crossword puzzle.

So, what did the outgoing, flamboyant Caitlin see in him? Simple. He adored her, worshipped the ground she walked on. He'd walk her to class, loan her his car with a full tank of gas, drop whatever he was doing to come at her beck and call. She knew, too, that underneath his bookish veneer was a driving ambition to be one of the nation's great professors of Eastern European history. She knew he would likely teach at Stanford or Harvard, and, sooner or later, his books and writings would be read around the globe. Now it was nearly so.

Caitlin had settled easily into the role of professor's wife. She felt comfortable in the world of academia. When she wasn't at home writing, she loved being on campus. She had yet another passion: Being the center of attention. She had made a science of drawing attention to herself: As the high school student body president, as editor of the college newspaper, as chairperson of the church outreach committee, as PTA president, as precinct representative. She played those roles for one purpose only: So that everyone would see and hear and know about Caitlin. Queen Caitlin. They would like her, admire her, envy her, want to be near her. They would strive to be part of her inner circle. And if not actually within her inner circle, to know somebody who was. Queen Caitlin and her Court. When she and Reggie entertained other professors and their spouses and assorted friends, she would treat him like her personal servant. "Reg, please bring me a glass of wine." Or "Reg, please run upstairs and get my new tennis racket so I can show it to our friends." Or "Reg, show these lovely people my new Russian oil painting." Or "Reg, where's your camera? Let's get some photos of all of us."

And because Reggie was crazy about her, he obeyed like a dutiful pawn.

When Caitlin became pregnant, you'd have thought it was the Immaculate Conception, the way she broadcast her pending motherhood. Before little Sabrina was born, Caitlin wrote to all her relatives and in-laws and friends and the alumni society and neighbors and anyone else she could think of to announce the name that she, Queen Caitlin, had chosen for her daughter. Reggie was amazed and quite annoyed at the cost of the announcements, over seven hundred, followed up with phone calls, most of which were long distance! And the baby showers that preceded Sabrina's birth; The Royal Family couldn't have been more elaborate: Catering services, gifts, flowers, balloons, home movies, musicians, fireworks!

As the years went by, Caitlin spared no expense to spin her web of influence. She formed a professor's wives club, whose purpose ostensibly was to raise money for charity and to do good works for the community. Its actual function was to surround Queen Caitlin with more adoring subjects. Oh, they raised money alright, mostly through silent auctions and bake sales at the student union and faculty lounge. But the donation checks usually went to a community group in which Caitlin was involved. The crowning moment was always when the local newspaper would send a photographer to snap a picture of The Queen presenting the donation check, and if the newspaper couldn't free up a photographer, she'd have a friend take a photo and then browbeat the editor mercilessly until the photo of The

Queen appeared in print.

"Well? Why not?" she often asked. "I didn't get a degree in mass communications for nothing!"

Thinking about her now, Reggie's jaw tightened until it hurt, as he pictured in his mind his conceited, selfish, self-serving, arrogant, spoiled, demanding wife. It's going to cost me a fortune, he thought, but I'm not sorry that she's no longer part of my life.

Chapter Twelve

There had been a few incidents on campus stemming from his makeup and hairstyle, which was part of Reggie's daily routine now. But one afternoon witnessed a particularly ugly scene. The Gay and Lesbian Alliance staged a march through campus, protesting a decision by the student council to not make a free meeting room available to the group; They would have to pay a minimal hourly fee. About 30 marchers, several with placards, moved across the campus and assembled on the lawn outside the student union. They were soon surrounded by a nondescript group who obviously opposed them, with shouts and signs of their own. Two of them held a makeshift gallows and a large sign that read "No More Dr. Thorne-types On Campus." Hanging from the gallows was a full-size mannequin with a blond wig and dressed in a woman's full-length dress. Pinned to the dress was a large paper sign that read, "Dr. Thorne," One of the marchers tried to knock the gallows down, but the two young men holding it stood their ground and held it up firmly. There was shoving and shouting and the mannequin swung crazily in the air. Then someone began throwing rocks at the mannequin and yelling, "No more queer professors! Stay in your closet!"

Reggie, lecturing at the time, missed the incident, but the campus newspaper and TV station both covered it and took photos. The hanging in effigy photo appeared in the campus newspaper. The TV footage somehow made it into the hands of the local CBS affiliate station and was broadcast on the evening news. Reggie and Malka were at home watching the six o'clock news when the shocking scene of the hanging mannequin filled the screen. It was an embarrassing and pathetic sight. Stunned and speechless, he watched the news story play out. Malka sat in silence, then she looked at him. "Why did they do that?" she asked. "Is that legal on campus?" Reggie didn't answer and turned his head away. "I mean, it's not like you're..."

He stood up and went into the kitchen. Malka heard the refrigerator door open. "Would you like a glass of wine?" he asked. She said no. She heard him pour a glass, drink it, and pour another. He came back, wine glass in hand, and sat down. For a long time, he said nothing. He stared at the TV, not really hearing it. He turned to look at Malka. "Why did they do it?" she asked again.

Reggie stood up and walked over to the large window that overlooked the back yard behind the apartment building. Two children were playing on the lawn near a concrete birdbath. The grass was thick and lush and needed mowing. Through the yard in an S-pattern was a gravel walkway. Along the perimeter of the yard were flower gardens with red and yellow and blue flowers. A large rose bush with big heavy red roses grew in the middle of the yard. For a long time, Reggie watched the children play with toy dump trucks and plastic blocks. One child would deliver blocks down the path where the other child waited with a yellow toy backhoe. The blocks were dumped out, then scooped up with the backhoe and moved back. This went on for at least a dozen deliveries that Reggie counted. Back and forth the trucks and blocks went. Then the mother of one of the kids came out with an Irish Setter. The dog bounded toward the children, its tail wagging. The children ignored the dog until its tail smacked one child in the face. The child rebuked the dog. "Sit your crazy dog," he said. The dog obediently sat near them, tail wagging, long liver-colored tongue hanging out. It sniffed the ear of one child, then licked it. "You crazy dog," the child said.

Malka came up behind him quietly and wrapped her arms around his waist and locked her fingers in front. His large hands covered hers. "What are you going to do?" she asked. Her voice sounded distant, eerie, beautiful, and almost angelic.

"I'm not going to do anything. There's nothing I can do. Nothing." The phone rang, and Reggie answered it. It was Dr. Hume, chairman of the history department. "Hello, Dr. Thorne, Rick Hume here." His first name was Roderick. He and Reggie weren't exactly on first-name basis, and it took him several seconds to realize who it was.

"Hello, Dr. Hume. Fine. Yes, I saw it." He paused. "Well, if you think it's necessary. Ok Dr. Hume. No, I'm fine. Thank you for calling. See you tomorrow."

There was a long silence after he hung up the phone. "Is everything ok?" Malka asked. He told her everything was ok, and security around the social science building would be increased. He doesn't want me to be intimidated by what happened today. He said he wasn't sure the students who carried the gallows are actually enrolled in classes, and the rock-throwing was completely out of order and dangerous, and he will make every effort to identify the participants and hold them accountable for their behavior.

Malka went into the kitchen, opened the fridge, took out the bottle of cold white wine and poured herself a glass. "Geez Reggie, sounds kinda scary having more security just so you can go to work."

Reggie nodded his head. "Yeah, I'm going to leave early, get to campus around seven, just stay in my office until my ten o'clock class. There's usually nobody around early in the morning."

"Would it help if I drove you? I could leave early." He looked at her. Good idea, he thought. They'd carpool over to campus together just in case his car was being watched.

That night, he lay awake thinking about all of it, trying to reason it all out. But sometimes it's better not to think too much. Sometimes there isn't a rational reason for everything. There may be a principle that controls or directs one's behavior, what is often referred to as rationale. But it isn't reasonably explainable. None of it made sense. But, somehow, all of it made perfect sense. After a while, he fell into a deep sleep.

Chapter Thirteen

The summer session lasted two more weeks. Several unpleasant incidents occurred. Reggie's car tires were flattened, so Malka got up early each day and dropped him off, then picked him up later. They discussed moving closer to campus. One Sunday, when he and Malka looked at a townhouse for rent near campus, the resident manager recognized Reggie and wasn't much interested in renting to him. He liked things quiet around the building, he said. Didn't want any problems. He thought the university had lost control.

Then there was the blackboard incident. The last Monday of the summer quarter, Malka dropped Reggie off early, and he went into the lecture hall to look at a new map of Germany that was installed over the weekend. When he got there, he noticed that someone had already pulled the map down. He rolled it up. Behind it, in large chalk letters, someone had written, "Dr. Drag, The Campus Fag; Dr. Slut, Hot Piece Of Butt; Dr. Bitch has Beaver Itch." He read it several times, then erased it thoroughly, then washed the entire blackboard with a wet sponge, then dried it with paper towels before going to his office.

There were four weeks before fall classes began, and Reggie had decided to get away for a few days and drive to the coast. He wanted to take Sabrina, but Caitlin vetoed the idea. She said he hadn't planned it far enough ahead. They would be out of town visiting friends and shopping for school clothes. Malka had tried to invite herself along, but he told her it wouldn't be a good idea since he was still legally married. Anyway he was sick of the messes she left around the apartment: Dirty clothes, dirty dishes, magazines on the floor, ice trays half full and left out on the counter to melt. He needed some time alone.

The morning he left for the coast, the air was cool and it felt like Autumn and the leaves were starting to turn. He stopped to top off the gas tank. Traffic was light as he headed out of town. The four-lane highway soon turned into one lane each way, and then the city disappeared in the rear view mirror and Reggie knew he was out of town and well on his way. Reggie thought about the surgery. No hospital or clinic in the United States offered the procedure. He would have to go to Toronto when the time came. It was coming pretty soon. He'd been in Toronto only once. He went to the World's Fair in Quebec, and spent three days in Toronto before returning home.

There was a low gray cloud cover and a strip of blue sky on the horizon. The shoulder of the highway was narrow and, in the ditch, grew a dense thicket of blackberries and cattails. He drove along through the countryside, farms on each side of the narrow highway and horses grazing in the pastureland. Then he pulled into a wayside park along a river. Seagulls circled overhead looking for scraps of food, and he knew he was getting close to the coast. The sun was trying to break through and he was glad to be out of the city and away from the university.

A state trooper was checking the park to see if anyone had been camping. He was questioning a young woman. "You've been parked here for a good part of the day, ma'am. You are aware that overnight camping is not allowed."

"Yes."

The trooper walked around her station wagon and looked in through the windows, then around to the back and checked her car license plate, while the young woman watched. The trooper was tall, and his brown uniform didn't fit. The collar was too big. He wore black western boots and was still talking to the young woman when Reggie drove off. He had reservations at the Sunset Lodge, an old four-unit hotel that seemed like it had been one large house originally. Each unit had a small kitchenette so he could fix simple meals, and it had a nice view of the beach and the ocean.

When he got there, he went in and spoke to the young woman, named Addie, who was the manager. She had a dark tan and wore cutoff jeans and a white blouse. "Nobody else is here, Mr. Thorne. You have the place to yourself. It's been very hot here for the last week." Reggie asked about the movie at the local theater. Addie handed him the local newspaper. "There's a movie guide on the back page. Also, your room has a VCR so you can rent a movie at the market. There's a coupon in your room for the rental."

Everything seemed all set, so after paying a three-night deposit, he went right up to his room. The front window was large and looked west out onto the beach and beyond to the Pacific. After he unpacked, he put on his swim trunks, grabbed a towel and went down to the beach. The beach was long and narrow, and the north end curved out in an arc. Out at the end of the point was a white lighthouse with a rust-colored roof above the window where the big spotlight was. The house next to it was also white with a similar roof. The sand was warm under his feet as he walked out. He waded ankle deep across the incoming tide, and the cold ocean water felt good after the long drive. He walked back to the dry beach, tossed his towel on the sand, then went back into the water quite a ways and dove under a breaker. The cold churning saltwater pummeled his body and turned him sideways under water. His head broke the surface. He took a very deep breath and dove down again, and swam under water with his eyes closed, then opened them to get his bearings. The saltwater stung his eyes and he blinked rapidly trying to get the saltwater out of his eyes. He couldn't see clearly. Standing up in waist-deep water, a wave broke over his shoulder and knocked him down. He stood up quickly and managed to steady himself in the rushing tide. His eyes were stinging painfully.

Off to his left a yellow frisbee floated by. Reggie retrieved it and looked toward shore and spotted two teenage boys looking at him. One of them waved at him. Reggie flipped the frisbee and one of the boys reached out and snatched it from its flight. "Thanks!" the boy shouted back. Reggie waved to him, then walked along through the water. His eyes were still stinging. Another breaker exploded behind him. He braced himself as the thrust of the water pounded against him. The late afternoon sun glistened off the water and he forgot about everything in his life except the ocean. A large jellyfish floated by, then another, then several smaller ones. The water was up to his stomach. The sun was beating down. Another larger wave broke to his left. He ducked under it and let it pass by and watched it roll up and flatten on the beach. He'd gone a couple hundred yards from where he left his towel. He walked up toward the dry sand, then jogged slowly back toward the frisbee players and found his towel and dried off and sat down. The hot sun felt good and he laid back and rested.

Later, he walked back to the hotel, showered, put on jeans and a pullover shirt and sandals, and combed his hair back in a ponytail, put on his designer sunglasses and went out and down the promenade toward the shops. At a wine shop, he found two local chardonnays, then continued down the strip. Up ahead a crowd of people were lined up for some reason. When he got there, he understood they were in front of the theater waiting for the box office to open. He worked his way around the line and walked further to a large round fountain with benches around it. The breeze coming in off the Pacific blew a fine spray from the fountain across his sunburned face and arms. He sat down and watched the people go by. Then a funny thing happened: Two young women and a young man, Reggie guessed college-age, came toward the fountain. They wore cutoff jeans and T-shirts. "I dare either of you to jump in," said the young man. The top of the fountain where the spouts were was about 12 feet above the sidewalk. Out of the spouts the water gushed in an arch and splashed into the large round pool below.

"I dare you," the young man said again. The girls were laughing and looking at the pool and the splashing water. Then one girl sat on the edge, spun around and her feet and lower legs were in the water. The young man came up behind her and pushed her, and in she went in a sort of sitting position, making a splash and letting out a shriek. The other girl laughed.

"Now you go in," the young man said.

"Why don't you?" she asked him. "Are you chicken?"

The young woman in the fountain tried to climb out but the young man pushed her back in. She grabbed his arm and pulled him, and he went in head first in a belly flop. Both girls were laughing. Then the other young woman stepped into the pool and stood under the cascading water like a shower. The three were laughing and splashing and making quite a spectacle with their wet T-shirts. Several people from the theater crowd came down and watched, laughing and shaking their heads at the foolishness in the fountain. Three younger boys on skateboards stopped and watched. They were looking at the wet T-shirts. One girl had large breasts and was wearing a bra. The other girl was smaller-chested and wore no bra, and her brown nipples were clearly visible through the wet T-shirt.

As he watched, Reggie was taken with their bravado, their flying in the face of the community norm. The three in the fountain looked at the growing crowd and were egged on and laughed and splashed all the more. "Hey, why don't all of you come in. Just jump in! "one of the girls shouted. The people laughed at her frivolity. All of a sudden, the three got out of the fountain and ran fast down toward the ocean waves. Reggie watched them for a moment until they disappeared behind a sand dune. His shirt was wet from all the splashing. He sat there for a while, then walked back to the hotel and went upstairs to his room. In one of the kitchen drawers he found a corkscrew and opened a bottle of wine, poured a glass and sipped it as he viewed the pounding surf, while the late afternoon sun sank slowly into the horizon.

Chapter Fourteen

In the morning it was foggy, and the Pacific Ocean was flat and gray, and the tide was low and there were no people on the beach but plenty of seagulls circling and checking the beach for scraps of food. Off in the distance a freighter slowly moved along the horizon, leaving a white plume of smoke behind it. Several fishing boats were working the coastline.

He put on a sweater and jeans and went barefoot down to the beach. Empty crab shells littered the sand. There were no frisbee players, but the seagulls were huddled with their backs to the wind and looking at Reggie in hopes of getting a scrap or two of bread. A young couple was standing way out on the tide flat. They both had long hair and wore heavy parkas against the cold.

He spent five days at the beach. The weather warmed up and it was perfect for long walks on the beach and swimming in the surf. The frisbee players came back. He went down to the theater and the fountain, but the wet T-shirt kids weren't around, and the movie didn't sound interesting, so he rented a couple films. One night, he went out to dinner at the only restaurant in town that had a view of the ocean and had a good meal and then stayed afterwards until it closed at midnight. It wasn't very busy, and the waitress sat down with him after a while and they talked. "I hate this place when business is slow," she said. "No tips. The chef is pissed off because he gets a percentage of the gross receipts. Not much money came through the door tonight."

"You live here in town?" he asked.

"Most of my life since I was eleven. I moved out a couple times, but I always come back. "

"Why?"

She shrugged her shoulders. "I don't know. It's familiar and comfortable most of the time. I pretty much know everyone in town. "Two young men came in and sat at the bar. "The bartender will be right back," she told them. "People don't move out here unless they're retired, or just want to live in a beach town and don't care about money. There are very few good jobs out here."

"Your family live out here?"

"My parents live in L.A., "she said. "They both work in the film industry." They sat there in silence for several minutes. Reggie looked out at the water. Floodlights beamed out from the restaurant across the breakers.

"Need a ride home?" he asked.

"Nope. I have a car."

"May I buy you a drink?"

"Can't. The boss doesn't want us drinking on the job. He really doesn't want us sitting with the customers."

Reggie nodded his head. "You live nearby?"

She looked at him. "Why? Are you hittin' on me now?"

He stood up. "No. Thanks for a nice supper." He stood up and headed toward the cashier.

"Take care, dude. What's your name?"

"Reggie."

"You can pay the bartender, Reggie. Stop in again. We serve a Sunday brunch."

The following morning, he was up early and after a quick cup of coffee, walked to the grocery market. He found a cart and was wheeling around the store and headed down the aisle marked cosmetics, and checked the lipsticks and mascara, reading the labels.

"Hi Reggie. I thought I recognized you. Buying lipstick this morning?"

It was the waitress from the restaurant last night. "Oh hi, no just picking up some food for dinner. "He was flustered and embarrassed. "What are you doing here?" It sounded like a dumb question.

"Same thing you're doing. Why don't you try on the lipstick. It might be a perfect shade." She removed a lighter shade from the rack, took off the top and handed it to him. "Or would you prefer a slightly lighter shade? Pink."

"What on earth are you talking about?"

She laughed. "I was only kidding! See you later." She left him holding the lipstick. He replaced the cap and returned it to the display rack.

"See you later." He steered the cart down toward the bakery aisle.

Chapter Fifteen

On the drive home, Reggie was worried that his roommate Malka had trashed the apartment. But he was looking forward to a happy reunion with his daughter. Two bottles of chardonnay and a rough draft of a manuscript were in the trunk.

When he got home, he was pleased and surprised that the place looked pretty decent. The voicemail had several new messages from Caitlin, Sabrina, his father, Dr. Saville and Rick Hume. He called Caitlin back. "The new pastor would like to meet with us, or just you alone, when you have time," she said.

"Concerning what?" Reggie asked.

Caitlin cleared her throat. "Our marriage. Our future. Church doctrine." They had been married in the church and both took the church seriously. "You need to be reminded of the severity of your personal behavior and its impact on our family, to say nothing of the university community. This is much bigger than you and me. I doubt you've given much thought to the ramifications of what you're doing with your life. You need to protect your good name and reputation, what's left of it." She handed the phone to Sabrina.

"Daddy! Please come over right now. I will tell you all about Berkeley." He told her another night this week would be better. Caitlin got back on the phone. "Let me know as soon as possible when you are willing to meet with the pastor. Bye." She hung up the phone.

Reggie called his dad and they talked for a few minutes. Then he called Rick Hume. "Good of you to call, Dr. Thorne. I thought you'd be interested to hear that the registrar's office told me all your classes this fall are full. Sold out! We'd like, if you're willing, to schedule another lecture, perhaps a Tuesday Thursday morning."

"Fine with me, Sir," Reggie said. "What do you make of it, Dr. Hume? The full classes?"

Hume chuckled. "Well, I believe there are a couple of factors. Your books and other writings draw a good deal of attention. And secondly, your name is associated with, shall we say, unorthodoxy. Many university students might enroll in your classes for no other reason than to see you up close."

There was a rather long silence. "Dr. Hume, this goes without saying, but I certainly hope the problems that occurred during the summer session aren't replayed this Fall." He was referring to the demonstration and hanging in effigy.

"Well, I think that's mostly up to you, Dr. Thorne. Don't you agree?"

"Sir, I respect you very much. If you are referring to my appearance and lifestyle, I must tell you it's not going to change. I've charted my course, so to speak."

"Dr. Thorne, I must confess I don't completely understand what's going on with regard to that. It might be wise for the two of us to meet soon to discuss this course you've charted. I feel certain that the two of us want the same thing for the university and the students and the alumni."

"I just want to teach, Sir. Teach and be free to live my life."

"Nobody on campus would deny you that," Broderick Hume said. "Will you be stopping by the department in the next few days?"

"Yes, in the morning. I'll come by your office when I get there."

"Very good. See you then, Dr. Thorne. Thanks so much for calling."

Then he dialed his psychiatrist, Collette Saville. She answered the phone on the first ring. "Hello Reggie, great to hear from you. How have you been?" He told her about his trip to the beach. "Good. Any revelations?"

"Full steam ahead. I've burned all my bridges."

"I'm just delighted to hear that, Reggie. I've given you a good deal of thought. I've decided to waive my usual fee. If you're willing, I'd like to resume our weekly visits. There will be no billing."

Reggie considered her offer. "How can you do that?"

"Let's call it an investment in my continuing education. I've learned a lot from you."

"I don't even have to think about it. I've enjoyed the sessions, and missed them recently."

"Good. Please call my office and schedule weekly appointments through the end of the year. I'll handle the billing." What she didn't tell him was that she intended to write her memoirs and use Reggie's case as the highlight of the book. Such a book, she thought, would draw international attention and open doors for her, TV and radio interviews and speaking engagements.

Later that evening, Reggie was almost asleep when the phone rang. Malka answered it. "Reggie, it's for you." He got out of bed and walked down the hall to the kitchen and took the phone from her.

"Reggie, this is Merrill Wells. Am I calling too late? I hadn't heard from you, so I decided to call. How are you?"

"I'm fine, Merrill, just fine. How are you and Bridget?"

"Very fine. We're having an end-of-summer barbeque next weekend. Would love to have you over."

"Which day, Saturday or Sunday?"

"The entire weekend," Merrill Wells said. "Most of the people will be there for two nights and days. You're welcome to stay over, too, if you like."

Reggie thought it over for a moment. "Tell you what, Merrill, for sure I'll be there Saturday afternoon and evening. Not sure right now about the sleepover. As you can guess, this is a very busy time of year for me, preparing for Fall classes."

"We'd enjoy your company if even for just a few hours."

Chapter Sixteen

The meeting with Rick Hume did not go well. It started out amicably, both of them drinking coffee and recalling pleasant experiences at the beach. Then things got intense. Reggie hadn't worn facial makeup, but he informed Hume that he intended to do so on a daily basis, and that he would wear feminine attire. Hume stood up from his chair. "Why?" he demanded to know in a frustrated tone of voice. "Why in the world can't all this be kept under wraps? "He shook his head. "I understand, as much as possible, your need to, as you put it, achieve gender reidentification. But can't you achieve it away from campus?" Hume was pacing back and forth in the spacious office.

"No more so than you can, Dr. Hume."

Hume threw his hands up in the air. "But I already have gender identification. I've been a male for fifty-one years, and I've never given it a second thought. It would never occur to me to show up to work dressed as a woman," Then he said as an afterthought, "unless it was Halloween." He laughed.

Reggie didn't laugh. He was uncomfortable but determined to get through this and make his point. He thought for a moment about having Collette Saville call Hume to explain. "Would it help if my psychiatrist called you?" He was sorry he said it. Hume shot him an icy stare.

"Your psychiatrist cannot rid this department or this university of the humiliation, the stain, brought on by your extremely odd behavior, Dr. Thorne." Hume stopped pacing and stood with his hands on his hips. "Now, you may be within your constitutional rights as an American to dress any way you like. But the university has rights too, as do the students and the alums." He was worked up and began pacing again and waving his arms. "To my knowledge, not one faculty member or student has agreed to be part of the laughing stock of American academia. I figure it's only a matter of time, Dr. Thorne, until you and this fine school are the butt of late-night TV jokes. If you ask me, I think we're damn lucky we haven't been lambasted on the cover of Mad Magazine!"

Now, for the first time, Reggie thought his job might be in jeopardy. He wanted to get the heck out of Hume's office. "Dr. Hume, it's clear we aren't likely to come to an agreement today. I have some work to do, so if you'll excuse me, please."

"Agreement!" Hume shouted. "What's to agree on? We hired Mr. Thorne and now it appears we are going to have Mrs. Thorne. I'm not sure but that you're in violation of your contract if you proceed with your 'gender redesignation'" Hume said mockingly. "I'm going to have the university legal office interpret this. This much I know: We have no agreement to employ Mrs. Thorne. What would your name become?"

"I don't know."

"We have no agreement to employ, and issue payroll checks to, a woman named Reggie Thorne. It may be that your transformation voids our contractual agreement, Dr. Thorne." Hume was pacing again. "Well, I have work to do also, Dr. Thorne. You may want to give this more very serious thought. You've got a brilliant career ahead of you. What are you, thirty-five?"

Reggie nodded. "That's right."

"Good luck with your classes. Dr. Thorne, and I mean that sincerely. You have students from all over the world enrolled." Reggie stood up and left.

Chapter Seventeen

Sabrina was wearing one of her new outfits when Reggie visited her after dinner. "Well, don't you look grown up, young lady," he said, hugging his daughter. Ironically, her outfit resembled what Reggie himself was wearing: Blue jeans, white turtleneck and brown leather sandals. Gone were the little girl dresses, the Mary Jane shoes, and the pigtails. My little girl now looks like a teenager, Reggie thought with some sadness.

"Come upstairs, Daddy. Look what else I got." He followed her upstairs and into her bedroom. She had laid out all her new clothes on her bed: Coveralls, leggings, blouses, flannel shirts, several new pairs of shoes, lots of socks, hairbands, and a new backpack and school supplies.

"Looks like you're all set," he said smiling. "But no dresses?"

Sabrina looked at her father doubtfully. "Daddy, I still have dresses and skirts from last year that I hardly ever wore, and they still fit kinda."

"You'll need a new winter coat."

"Mom and me looked at some yesterday. I don't need it yet Daddy."

Caitlin entered the room wearing a white kaftan. "Hi Reg. How does it?"

"I'm fine. You've been to the Levant, I see."

"Better the Levant than Sodom," she said curtly. She turned

and walked out of the room. "Would like a word with you before you leave," she said over her shoulder.

On Sabrina's wall was a new poster with illustrations of species of whales. Reggie looked at it closely. "We got that at Tower Books in Berkeley. Do you like it? You can have it for your apartment."

Reggie turned to her and hugged her. "It's for your room, Sabrina. You keep it."

"But Daddy, if you want it, you can put it on the wall next to your bed to remind you of me."

From her earliest days, she and her father had been close. She was not only bright and beautiful, but she was also fun to be with. The bike rides, the camp outs, the playing together in the university swimming pool. He taught her how to swim, to dive, to bike-ride. What a great memory he had of the bike-riding lessons. When Sabrina was five, she was ready to make the move from tricycle to two-wheeler. The training wheels that her dad had bolted onto the new Christmas bike only frustrated the daring, competitive, brave young Sabrina. After seeing other children riding bikes without the support of the extra rear wheels, she begged her dad to remove them. Reluctantly, he did so.

Early one Saturday morning, Sabrina was ready for her first lesson on her two-wheeler. They stood there with the red bicycle at the edge of an outdoor basketball court. "Ok, now I'll run along with you for a while. You steer the bike. Don't look at the pedals. Just look straight ahead and steer. I'll be right here next to you." He began to run along slowly as she pedaled. She was scared and whimpered. She was beginning to understand balance and steering and freedom.

"Don't let go Daddy," she pleaded, knowing that he would let go eventually, that he had to let go for her to learn. He ran alongside her, gripping the back of the bicycle seat, holding it upright, Sabrina pedaling, the wind in her beautiful, thick, dark hair, her eyes and face excited and fearful and full of life and learning and beginning to understand how to balance and ride on her own.

Holding the bike seat, Reggie ran as fast as he could in a large oval around the court until he was winded and could run no more and had to let go. His daughter pedaled and didn't look back, and she did not know for several seconds that her father was twenty feet behind her. She glanced quickly over her shoulder and realized he wasn't there, but his voice was there. "Look straight ahead, Sabrina. You're doing fine! Steer!" He summoned the last bit of energy he had and sprinted up alongside her. "You're doing it! You're riding the bike all by yourself! You're a very good bike-rider." She smiled into the wind. She understood. She rode and rode that day, in circles, in figure eights, off the basketball court, across the playground, over a strip of grass and back around. When she pedaled past her father, she had on her face a look of pure satisfaction and victory and success. He stood and watched her maneuver the bike with agility and grace. She was, he thought, the most wonderful child on Earth.

Now, standing there in her bedroom, he very much wanted the whale poster. He carefully removed the push pins and rolled the poster into a tube. "Here's a rubber band, Daddy," she said, slipping the elastic into place.

On his way out, he stopped briefly in the kitchen to see Caitlin. "You can expect to receive the divorce papers in the next few days" she said. "You've certainly fucked things up royally."

Chapter Eighteen

The sessions with Dr. Saville started up again. At their first meeting, Reggie told her about being seduced by his roommate Malka. "Honestly, I was surprised by how turned on I was with her," he said. "What are your thoughts on the matter?"

Collette Saville smiled and thought for a moment. "Are you asking me what I think clinically or romantically?"

"Both."

She pushed herself back in her chair and crossed her legs. "People differ in their feelings about sex and romance, regardless of sexual or gender orientation. And people change as time goes on. What you are today and who you are today is not the same as ten or fifteen years ago or even a year ago. You'll experience more changes yet." She stood up and walked to the service counter and poured two glasses of water from a green ceramic pitcher and handed one to Reggie. "In a recent sociological study, it was noted that the link between sexual preference and sexual identity isn't completely clear. "She took a drink. "But one thing is clear: Your male sex drive is still part of your life biologically. But don't let it be a source of confusion or frustration."

Reggie nodded his head. "What's weird, though, is I didn't have a climax. Malka did, twice."

Collette Saville laughed. In the back of her mind, though, she was concerned about this heterosexual dalliance. She hoped he would keep his mind off heterosex. She would minimize the importance of a one-nighter and, instead, keep him focused on his transsexualism, his female identification, and his upcoming estrogen treatments. She would emphasize how proud she was of his strength and determination in the face of very unpleasant obstacles, none of which were of his own making. As his psychiatrist, she was entering perhaps the most important phase of her career. Dr. Reginald Thorne was, in a manner of speaking, her goose that would lay her golden egg. Her job now was to support and guide his persuasion that nature had made a terrible, cruel mistake and she would help him correct it. Colette Saville knew, better than her patient, that his complete transition would present very difficult conflicts that went well beyond any problems he'd had up until now.

The sexual preference issue, for example. Reggie was thirty-five years old. For most of those years, society and his family had directed him in his heterosexual male role, and he had played the role quite well. Good-looking and virile as a teenager, he was popular with girls who spent lots of time at the library. He dated as often as he wanted, which was one or two weekends a month. He had avoided most sports, pursuing instead student politics, school newspaper staff, editor of the yearbook, and captain of the debate team. Occasionally he played golf. Most of his friends played football and basketball.

When it came to girls, Reggie's parents had one concern: In high school, he was a little too girl-crazy. He'd spend an hour every evening on the phone talking to a girl. He'd go to the beach and, while he was reading a book, look at the young ladies in their swimsuits. He even had a pinup in his closet before his mom found it and removed it. Just be careful, his parents said. Always carry a condom. So, he did. Word got around school that Reggie was always prepared. Every time he went out on a date, the lucky girl he dated was surrounded the next day by friends, all wanting to know what happened. Was Reggie prepared? One girl asked, "Did Reggie peel the banana?" Usually, the question was met with a giggle and a guarded denial that admitted more than it denied. One girl said bluntly, "Let me put it this way: I'd take Reggie Thorne's muscle any day over all the muscle on the varsity football team. He knows how to flex it." He was branded the Campus Stud, the quiet, studious type. He was never one to boast, the girls whispered to one another. He does his boasting with his dick. His acceptance into Princeton served to heighten his attractiveness. This guy is going places, the girls all said.

When Reggie came home on Christmas break, his phone rang constantly, mostly calls from young women. He had arranged to work full-time at a local bookstore during the two-week break, but after four days, the store manager let him go. Said he needed a real live wire to help out during the Christmas rush. Reggie had been staying out most of the night and would show up to work the following morning dog-tired, spaced out, hung over, and barely able to make it through the day. So, he was fired. Without the bookstore job, he could sleep all day and screw around at night. His parents, though disappointed, said very little. "You're only young once," his dad said. "He's having fun. He'll be back to school soon and hitting the books."

Reggie was definitely having fun. Without a job, his pocket money dried up fast, but it didn't slow him down. A high school friend named Monica Beck called him and told him, "No problem if you have no money, Reggie. I have money and a car. Let me take you out." And she did! She picked him up in her VW Beetle. When he got into the tiny car, he wondered how he would take her. But she had already figured it out. They parked behind the high school and quickly climbed in the back and rocked that little car till Reggie thought they'd break the springs.

A couple days later, after the Christmas Eve church service, another former classmate, Rebecca Bollinger, slipped a note into Reggie's suit pocket. He went into the men's room and read the note: "Please call me. Great to see you at home." The day after Christmas he called her. Her family was out of town for several days, she said, and would he like to come over for a swim? They never made it to the pool. Using the old line, "You've never actually seen my house," she led the gleeful, horny Reggie back toward the bedrooms. Beats the heck out of doing it in a VW, Reggie thought. He was there most of the night. He wondered where this seventeen-year-old church girl learned all her tricks, but it didn't really matter. All that mattered was she was willing and eager to do anything he wanted. Her slender, supple body could bend into the most remarkable positions! The next morning, as the December sun rose, Reggie took the bus home and slept all day.

Reggie's early manhood was spent learning and practicing the lines for his natural hetero role. He was a gifted performer, and in each act, each scene, he stepped up center stage. He was, or so it seemed, a natural for the male role. Even now, he seemed attracted to women, which could present a problem for Collette Saville. Reggie would have to desire a relationship with a man in order to prove that he was, in fact, a born-again woman. Moreover, this interest in the opposite sex was one prerequisite to approving a patient for genital surgery. Thus, Collette Saville gave more than a passing interest to Reggie's one-nighter with Malka. She was troubled by the fact that Malka got turned on by Reggie, for which he deserved at least some of the credit. Well, she thought, this Malka gal may just be a horny little bitch with a hair-trigger clit. Maybe she'd get herself off with any stray dog that happened along. Still, the way Reggie told it, he and Malka had been doing it for a good 30 minutes, which meant his male organs were working just fine.

Collette Saville was troubled by Reggie's ability to perform. Then again, she knew that the estrogen treatments would greatly reduce his ability in that area. His testicles would atrophy, and his libido would diminish. She decided to move up the estrogen therapy by several weeks.

Chapter Nineteen

Although Reggie and Malka had shared a tumble that night, it had been over a year since Caitlin Thorne had bedded down with her husband. At first, she was confused by his inattention. She wondered if it was caused by something she'd said or done. She finally decided he was simply working too hard. He was physically and mentally strained and tired. No part of it was her fault, she reasoned. The simple fact was that her husband's career was pulling him in too many directions at once, and there was nothing left for her. This happens, though, when you're married to a Type-A personality, she rationalized. He teaches full-time, he writes, he advises government leaders, he spends time guest lecturing out of town. And that pest of an agent of his won't leave him alone, always calling and wanting another manuscript or asking him to do more book signings.

So, Caitlin jumped headlong into her freelance writing and charity work and art collecting. One day, though, Caitlin had found a pair of white silk panties in the pocket of one of Reggie's sport coats. She'd been getting some clothes together to take to the dry cleaners and happened upon them. Her first thought was another woman. With a calm voice, she confronted her husband that evening. "I found these," she said, waving the underpants. "They're not mine." She was quite surprised when his reply was delivered in an equally calm voice.

"They're mine."

She laughed nervously. "Yours?"

"Yes, I wear them."

Caitlin held the panties to her nose and smelled them. They didn't smell like a woman. "You have a drawer full of underwear. Why in the world would you wear these?"

"I like them."

She looked at him quizzically. "Ok. Any more surprises I should know about?"

"No. "

But there were. One day Caitlin borrowed Reggie's car because hers was in the shop. She was feeling around under the seat for the lever to move the seat forward. She found a bra. It had small cups and obviously was not hers. She also found two lipsticks, a compact and mascara in the glove compartment. Later that day, she drove to the university to pick him up. She put the bra and makeup on the passenger seat so he couldn't miss it. It was quite a little scene when he opened the car door to get in.

"Let's don't play games, Ok. If you're sleeping with another woman, I figured you'd be smart enough to keep her shit out of your car!" She was almost shouting. The car windows were down, and people were gathering outside and listening. Caitlin was gripping the steering wheel.

"Drive, would you please," he said, "and stop shouting. I don't have a girlfriend. Those things are mine."

She glared at him. "I'm not driving anywhere until you tell me what the hell is going on." Now she was shouting.

"Pipe down Caitlin. Let's just go home. These things are mine."

"I thought you liked women with big boobies. This little bra isn't big enough..."

He interrupted her. "It's mine, and it fits!"

She slammed the gearshift into first and peeled out of the parking lot. "Catlin, go easy on my car, will you please!" She held the accelerator to the floor as the car lurched forward.

"Whatever you're up to, I'm going to get to the bottom of it. If you're shagging babes while you're out of town, you're going to be sorry." She was fuming. He had never seen her so mad.

"There are no other babes." He decided it was time to spill the beans. "I like to wear women's clothes from time to time. It's a change of pace."

Caitlin was driving along the boulevard in the rush hour traffic. "A change of pace?"

"Yes." The traffic had slowed down to a crawl.

After several minutes of silence, she asked, "Would you mind telling me what the hell is going on?"

"It's simple. I enjoy wearing women's clothes. I've wanted to for the past few years, and now I'm doing so."

She flashed him a quick glance. "When are you doing this?"

"Mostly when I'm out of town. In my hotel room. Two weeks ago in San Diego, I bought a nice outfit and wore it all evening in my hotel room."

"Where is the outfit now?"

"I threw it away. I knew I couldn't bring it home, so I tossed it in a dumpster." Then he said something that really shocker his wife. "Right now, I'm wearing panty hose."

"Holy shit!" she said in almost a whisper. The relationship, which had been slowly going downhill, suddenly began careening out of control. Caitlin refused to allow the cross-dressing at home. What made matters worse was she began imagining that she was missing underwear, and she accused Reggie of taking it, which in fact he was not. She began seeing a psychiatrist. She was more than turned off by her husband's behavior. It made her physically ill. She lost weight and their sex life came to a halt. Although she was successful at keeping her husband's secret from her daughter, the strain of worrying about it was eating her alive.

When Reggie told her one day that he was beginning gender modification, she showed him the door. There was simply no way she was going to share her home with him. The marriage was over. "You lose, creep!" she told him. "I want your perverted ass out of my house."

Chapter Twenty

The barbeque at the home of Merrill and Bridget Wells was a doozie. He couldn't remember ever seeing that much wine consumed in one place. Himself a light drinker, Reggie mostly stayed to the side and watched. He also skipped the overnight invitation. Merrill and Bridget had assembled an unbelievable assortment of people. A good many were planning to make a weekend of it. The dirt road leading up to the Wells' residence was packed with vehicles of all descriptions: Pickup trucks, some with campers, sports cars, expensive foreign sedans, motorcycles, a dune buggy, a station wagon without a top, and a perfectly restored red 1958 Chevrolet Impala. Reggie had to park a long way away and walk up the hot, dusty road.

The house was packed with guests. Reggie lost count at seventy. The steady stream of people made it impossible to get an accurate head count. He asked Bridget how many guests she expected. "Around 200."

"Good grief. What if they all show up?"

"Well, we've booked rooms at local motels. We can accommodate about twenty in the house and guests can toss their sleeping bags on the lawns. It'll be ok."

"Bridget, may I ask you a personal question?" She nodded her head yes. "Is Merrill confused about who he is?"

"No. Are you?"

"Yes."

It was mighty hard to figure out what gender they all were. A woman who resembled a well-known magazine publisher turned out to be a male college basketball coach in his gender identification stage. Another lady with short red hair was a transsexual who had not had genital surgery and was working as a call girl to earn money for the reconstruction surgery. Bridget stood with Reggie and pointed out most of the transsexuals in the crowd. As the evening wore on, Reggie wandered outdoors for a breath of fresh air. It smelled like late summer. Stars filled the dark blue sky. There was definitely the feel of Autumn in the air.

Over near the 1958 Chevy Impala, two men were smoking a joint. Reggie walked over, and one of the men passed the joint to him. Reggie declined. The two guys were checking out the perfect red paint job and the chrome reverse rims. "Is this your car?" one of them asked Reggie.

"I wish it was." He walked back toward the house. Bridget met him at the door.

"Did you introduce yourself to those two?" she asked.

"No. We were just admiring that old Chevy. I didn't catch their names."

"They're both transsexuals. Two years ago, they were both gals. One of them has had difficulty after the surgery. She had the procedure at a clinic in Toronto, but there are problems now. "

"What sort of problems?"

"He can't get a lasting erection."

"How do you know all this?"

Bridget explained that her husband knows both of them quite well. They told him, she said. Reggie glanced back at the two men, one of whom was sporting a full beard.

Chapter Twenty-One

The Fall quarter was always a busy time for the professors. Reggie's classes for Fall and Winter were full, and the Spring classes were nearly so. The prep time for each class was extensive. Contemporary European History 350 is how they were listed in the catalog. There was also a 400 series lecture for seniors majoring in either history or political science, and a graduate level class on the history and politics of the Soviet Union. All of his students were either upperclassmen or grad students. He worked long hours on the final draft of his new book. The week of Thanksgiving, he attended a memorial service in Washington D.C. for a group of United Nations employees who were shot to death in Rwanda while investigating human rights violations.

While he was there, he gave two lectures at Georgetown University on the political aims of Socialists and Communists in Bulgaria. Later, he had dinner with the Undersecretary of State for European Affairs. Reggie reluctantly declined a staff offer, citing his contractual agreement with the university. "You'd make a fine ambassador, Dr. Thorne. If the opportunity presents itself, is there any chance you could take a leave of absence to serve?"

"It would be foolish of me to close the door altogether. Let's agree that I'll leave it ajar for the present. You've got my phone number. If the President calls, it would be hard to say no." But as they were talking, Reggie knew it would be impossible for him to work for the President. All ambassador posts require senate confirmation. His personal life, including the psychiatric counseling, divorce, and cross dressing, would be made public by the media, and embarrass the President and the university. His friend, the undersecretary, was not aware of his transsexuality. That evening, his hair was covered by a short wig, and he wore no makeup.

But he knew that senate confirmation was impossible. There was also the issue of the estrogen treatments that had begun a few months earlier. He was already feeling the effects. No, working in the diplomatic corps, once a career option, was now out of the question.

When he returned home from Washington, D.C., his roommate Malka was having a small dinner party. He walked in just as they were having dessert, and she invited him to join them. Just then, the phone rang. It was Caitlin and she was in a bitchy mood. "Well, Reg, it turns out that one of our neighbors here is taking night classes at the U. You're the talk of the neighborhood! I can't tell you how many of our neighbors wonder what Sabrina's father is up to, running around looking for all the world like the swishiest little pansy this side of the Castro. 'Here comes Sister Honeypot Limpwrist, sashaying around like a good little fairy.'"

Reggie changed the subject. "I was offered a staff position in the State Department."

Caitlin was on a roll. "I bet that's not the only position you were offered. Obviously, the President doesn't know about your little closet queen game."

He was shaking with anger. "Are you about finished?"

"No! I hope you realize that Sabrina and I are going to have to move out of town, thanks to you and your pervert bullshit! We're not going to stay around here and suffer humiliation every day. You have no idea, do you, what you've done to our lives. It's atrocious! Do you even care? I mean, why don't you just get yourself off with some hot slut?"

"I'll speak to Sabrina about my lifestyle changes."

"The hell you will! If I had my way, you'd never say another word to that poor child. Go to hell!" With that, she hung up.

Chapter Twenty-Two

The Fall quarter came to an end. During finals week, many of the male students did something extraordinary one morning. Reggie always liked to enter the lecture hall a few minutes late, after most of the students were seated. He walked in and glanced at the full seats. Nearly all the male students were dressed in drag. Blond and red wigs, facial makeup, dresses, and brassieres stuffed with who-knows-what. It was quite a sight. He was stunned. Then the class, nearly 100 strong, stood up and applauded. When the clapping stopped, a male student in drag walked up to the podium and handed Reggie a scroll. He unrolled it. In large Old English lettering it read: "We, your unworthy subjects, declare this day a national holiday: Dr. Reginald Thorne Day. Regarding European History, we've learned much. Regarding a great American virtue, courage, no lesson or lecture or textbook could teach us what you, by example, have imparted to us. We shall never forget you." It was signed by each student.

Reggie laughed. "Thank you. No, I'm not giving you all A's. So, sit down, get out your pens and bluebooks, while I pass out the exams." Then he distributed the tests.

The weeks went by, and Reggie's appearance changed radically. He was fully into the gender reorientation phase, dressing and living as a woman at home, on campus, and socially. The genital reconstructive surgery was scheduled for early winter in Canada. Colette Saville's life changed too, with the publication of her memoirs, which drew national attention, and brought her the celebrity she sought. Despite feeling betrayed by her, Reggie continued the counseling sessions, because without them the surgery would not be performed. Malka told him she was thinking of writing a book called "The Night I Shagged A Tranny."

After her divorce was final, Caitlin began dating an art dealer who persuaded her not to move. But Sabrina was sent to a boarding school on the other side of the state. The university somewhat reluctantly went along with Reggie's transformation, and after a while most of the staff just accepted it. Dr. Hume hired a part-time secretary to help Reggie manage his busy schedule of guest lectures and book signings. The clerk at the Department of Motor Vehicles just shrugged when Reggie came in to have his driver's license changed. A new photo was taken, and the M was replaced with an F. "We do these sex change things more often than you might think," the clerk said.

One cold December evening, Regina Thorne boarded a plane for Toronto, where her surgery would be done the following day.

www.ingramcontent.com/pod-product-compliance
Lightning Source LLC
LaVergne TN
LVHW020431080526
838202LV00055B/5132